by Margaret D. Gallo
illustrated by Christian Slade

SCHOOL PUBLISHERS

Printed in China

ISBN 10: 0-15-377361-8
ISBN 13: 978-0-15-377361-7

Ordering Options
ISBN 10: 0-15-377148-8 (Grade 4 Collection)
ISBN 13: 978-0-15-377148-4 (Grade 4 Collection)
ISBN 10: 0-15-377848-2 (package of 5)
ISBN 13: 978-0-15-377848-3 (package of 5)

2 3 4 5 6 7 8 9 10 0940 17 16 15 14 13 12 11 10 09

It was the beginning of summer vacation in 1948, and the Sawyer kids were sitting on the front steps. Jeb Sawyer, who had just turned twelve, was keeping an eye on his younger brother and sister.

"What do you want to do?" Mickey asked his older brother.

"I don't know, what do you want to do?" replied Jeb. "How about you, Margie?"

Margie just smiled broadly because at six years old, she was just plain thrilled to be hanging out with her older brothers. Jeb was about to suggest that they play catch when something in the distance caught his eye.

A medium-size dog with long, floppy ears and a red coat was trotting up the driveway. The dog walked up to the children, sat down, and began to wag its tail.

"Where do you think he came from?" exclaimed Mickey.

"He must belong to someone around here. Quick, Mickey, go get Mama," said Jeb.

Mama came to the porch, and the dog went to her, wagging its tail all the while. Mama patted him and said, "I wonder where you live. You don't seem to have a tag."

"Can we keep him, Mama?" begged Margie.

"No, Pumpkin, we need to find out where he belongs," replied Mama.

Mama found a rope and tied it around the dog's neck like a leash. All that afternoon, Mama and the children walked the dog from one neighbor's house to another. At each house, they asked whether the dog lived there.

No one had ever seen the dog before or even knew of a missing pet. Finally, the little group went back and sat down on the porch. The dog jumped up next to Mama and settled right down, as if he belonged there.

"It certainly seems like he likes it here," observed Mickey.

"Can we keep him now, Mama?" asked Margie.

"Let's wait and see," answered Mama.

That night, when Papa came home from work, he was greeted by a strange dog on the porch. When the dog saw Papa coming up the walk, he jumped up and wagged his tail, greeting Papa like he had known him forever. Puzzled, Papa walked into the house, and Mama explained how the dog had just showed up on the porch.

"Papa, can we please keep him?" asked Margie.

"Dogs are just too much work and too much responsibility. We'll find the owners, or we'll have to find a new home for the dog."

Then Papa and Mama went into the kitchen to get dinner ready. Mama talked to Papa about the dog.

"It would be good for the children to learn how to care for an animal," Mama said to Papa.

Now Papa, being very prideful, did not always let people see what a soft heart he had.

"What if the kids get attached to the dog and then the owners show up?" Papa thought to himself. "What if I get too attached to the dog?"

Papa recalled that he never had a dog when he was a kid because his sister had an allergy to pet fur. He had always longed for a dog.

Eventually, Papa said, "Let's try to find the owners, and then we'll see what happens."

The next day the family made some signs. Each sign consisted of the dog's description and the family's address. Papa and the kids posted the signs all over town, and they called the police, the town hall, and the animal shelter. No one had reported a lost dog. It was as if the dog had appeared out of thin air.

A week went by, and still no one came for the dog. Every night, the dog would lie at Papa's feet while he read. The dog would wait for the kids or Mama on the porch. The dog clearly felt like a part of the family.

Finally, Jeb declared, "It looks like no one wants the dog but us."

"Yes, Papa, I think this dog wants to stay with us," Mickey piped up.

"Please, Papa, now can we keep him?" begged Margie.

"All right," said Papa, "but the dog is here on a trial basis. If he intends to stay here, he has one week to prove himself. If he acts up, then we'll have to find him another home. You must all take turns feeding him and walking him. If anyone complains, the dog goes. We'll need to make him a bed to sleep in, too."

The next day, the children found a cardboard box and made it cozy with an old blanket.

"Here you go, boy, here's your new bed," said Jeb. The dog jumped right in, snuggled up, and settled down.

That afternoon, they left the dog out in the yard. He was still a young dog who could get into plenty of mischief.

When Jeb came out, he noticed Papa's prize tomatoes lying about. "Uh-oh, we better fix this up before Papa sees what the dog did."

The children replanted the tomato plants and then gathered the loose, green tomatoes. They gave them to Mama, who put them aside to make a sauce.

The next day, the children taught the dog to bring Papa his slippers at night. As usual, Papa sat down to read after dinner. Jeb handed the slippers to the dog, who snatched them up and trotted right over to Papa. Papa felt his heart melt. "Good dog," he said, patting him on the head.

The dog seemed to take a liking to Papa's slippers, however. The very next day, Margie found the dog happily chewing away on one slipper. "Oh, no, look at Papa's slippers!" Margie exclaimed.

"Don't worry," Mama told her children, and she went over to a closet and dragged out an enormous box.

Papa never liked to get rid of anything, especially old slippers. Mama put the chewed up slipper into the box and took an old slipper out of it. It looked almost identical to the one the dog chewed. "Good thing Papa is about ready for a new pair of slippers," Mama said.

That night, the dog brought Papa his slippers again. "Good dog," said Papa and promptly put on his slippers. He stared at the left slipper because something was funny about it, but he paid it no mind and went back to reading. From the doorway, the children breathed a sigh of relief.

The children kept a keen eye on the dog all week long. They cleaned up the broken vase that the dog's tail knocked over, and they wiped his muddy footprints from the kitchen floor.

Finally, the week was over, and it was time to decide about keeping the dog. That night, Papa came home and declared, "If this dog is going to be a member of our family, we should really give him a name."

All at once, the children whooped with joy. The dog, knowing that something big had just happened, wagged his tail and barked.

That night, each member of the family made a list of names, and then Papa took the lists. "We'll select a few names and then take a vote," he decided. Papa read through some names, but no one could agree.

"What about Rusty?" Papa said, looking at the dog's pretty red coat. Secretly, Papa had always wanted a dog named Rusty.

"Oh, Papa, I love it!" said Margie, clapping her hands.

Jeb went over to the dog and bent down. "What do you think, Rusty, do you want to stay here with us?" Rusty's tail thumped happily because he had found a home!

Think Critically

1. Why doesn't Papa want a dog?

2. Why does Mama hide the slipper in the box?

3. Do you think this story is realistic? Explain why or why not.

4. When did you first think that Papa would agree to keep the dog? Read aloud the part that made you think that.

5. Do you think Papa would have kept the dog if he had known the dog dug up his garden and made a mess in the house?

 Social Studies

Make a Chart This story takes place in the 1940s. The family had to make signs by hand when today we would just make them on the computer. Find out more about the time when this story took place. Make a chart to show how life was different then from now.

School-Home Connection Ask family members and friends what they think a person needs to do when caring for a pet. Make a list from their suggestions.

Word Count: 1,269 (1,273)